Trade Like a Pro

20 Winning Stock Market Strategies That Will Make You Rich

Table of Contents

Introduction

There is no doubt that in these times of economic uncertainty some people are turning away from the stock market, while others are turning toward it as a place to ensure financial stability or even outright wealth.

It is not as difficult as you might think to earn a substantial living in the market if you know where to look for useful advice. If you want to know how to trade like a pro even if you are a novice to the investment world, turn to technology.

One can't just trade with stocks without even knowing stock trading strategies. If you need stock investment advice for playing the stock market lucratively, keep on reading. If you are thinking of where to invest your hard earned money, why not try to trade with stocks?

Playing the stock market means offering and purchasing stocks. A stock investment advice you should not miss out on, however, is to be prepared to face risks, and, that there is no guarantee that you'll earn profit or won't lose your money.

In this book "Trade Like a Pro - 20 Winning Stock Market Strategies That Will Make You Rich" I am going to look into various winning stock market strategies that you need to know before plunging into the stock market business.

Before doing that, let us look into some areas of stock market investment.

Chapter 1

Three Different Types of Traders

Being called a day trader, swing trader, or position trader is both a badge of honor and a title. The majority of traders entering the field come through one of these gateways. Depending on the book they've read or the guru they're following at the time, a trader can feel a sense of belonging.

The problem with being a "time frame specialist" is that it holds you back. While any time frame may earn you money, there are times when the market dictates which time frame is better. By not listening to the market and insisting instead on trading a specific time frame, you lose opportunities for profits and limit your success.

The market is the great dictator of time frame decisions. To ignore the market's rhythms is to make it difficult to let your profits ride and cut your losses as necessary. Being a time frame specialist can limit your chances to manage your losses.

Various loss strategies that apply to one time frame can apply to another time frame, if the trader is willing to look beyond his horizon.

That being said, there are three traditional time frame categories that most traders fall into: day, swing, and position. No time frame is superior to another. They each have their own pros and cons.

The secret to being a pro in successful trading is to move from one time frame to another seamlessly (if it makes sense), and knowing when it makes sense to do so.

Day Trader

Investopedia defines day trader as, "A stock trader who holds positions for a very short time (from minutes to hours) and makes numerous trades each day. Most trades are entered and closed out within the same day."

The name could be day trader, scalper, or active trader, but the process is the same. You execute trades intraday in order to achieve your profit goals, with the express purpose of being flat in your trading at the end of the day.

Whether you are attempting to earn a few hundred dollars or even thousands, the practice is to take many small chances throughout the day without risking all your capital.

By minimizing how much you are trying for, whether it's a few points on the Emini S&P or a couple hundredths of a cent in currency trading, the belief is that you are risking less and therefore will have much greater longevity than the swing or position traders.

On the surface, this logic is sound. Problems arise when the market significantly moves against you when you least expect it, or when slippage occurs, or when there is a spread involved in the quoted bid ask price.

Any of these three situations can diminish how much you are able to make and at the same time how much you are losing.

Couple this with a trader's need to be right about the markets - as opposed to being profitable - and you run into what could be characterized as slow death. Every day the trader is gaining a little, but losing more.

As time goes on he finds his account value slowly eroding, until eventually he either has no more trading capital or he can't make any headway.

In the end the demise of the day trader comes about because of two things: time and commissions. Since day trading is supposed to save you money with a diminished time frame, it inversely requires more of your time to monitor, prepare, and participate.

For those who simply want to make a little extra money or for those who are looking to supplement their retirement, the commitment can easily far exceed the rewards. Spending 10 to 12 hours a day involved in the markets, while mentally stimulating, can make anyone's retirement feel like a chore.

The second failure of the day trader comes by way of commissions. Now even E*TRADE has jumped on the bandwagon and joined the futures revolution by offering 99-cent commissions. Commission rates are playing limbo around the world, to actively recruit futures and forex traders.

The problem is that no matter how low they go, they will always beat the customer. You have to think of the commodities house as a bookie joint.

No matter what side the customer is on, long or short or whether he wins or loses, the brokerage makes money. And the dirty little secret of the industry is the fact that the lower the commissions, the more the customers will trade.

Like anything in life, if you think that you are getting a deal for something you buy regularly, you simply buy more of it. That's how Costco and Sam's Club work. Those two companies are continually making record-breaking profits.

There is no material difference between how these retail outlets generate business and trading. The perceived discount in trading encourages the traders to trade more. Does this mean that there is less slippage or that the market is less likely to move against you?

Not only have all your risks stayed the same, but you have increased your exposure to them simply because it seemed cheaper to do so.

One of the most influential studies on the topic, "Do individual day traders make money?" (Brad M. Barber et al., 2004), took a serious look at the day trading phenomena by analyzing 130,000 investor accounts.

Their abstract put forth many straightforward conclusions, one of which was, "Heavy day traders earn gross profits, but their profits are not sufficient to cover transaction costs." This is an alarming revelation. If you are solely a day trader, you are not working for yourself: You are working for the brokerage.

Swing Trader

Investopedia defines a swing trading as, "A style of trading that attempts to capture gains in a stock within one to four days."

The level of research that has been conducted on day trading simply doesn't exit for swing trading. The flexibility of the time frame means that a trader may hold onto a trade for a few days or a few weeks, depending on the end goal.

Like their day trading counterparts, swing traders attempt to gain a few hundred dollars or more and they also attempt to limit their exposure to the markets by minimizing the amount of time spent in the trade.

There is the assumption that the market moves in a particular direction, whether up or down, for only a finite amount of time before it retraces or pulls back.

The role of the swing trader is essentially to pick when the move begins and to get out right when the move ends. This ability is akin to being able to pick market highs and lows. The swing trader is looking to find out when the market is going to explode on fundamental or technical information and how much of a profit they can gain while it is moving.

This is nearly an impossible task to undertake. Many swing traders tend to be system or black-box traders. They look for the market to be packaged as a black-and-white scenario of "get in here and exit there."

The problem with this style of trading is that its predictive nature can lead to a lot of false entries and exits. You can be fooled by false entry signals or exit trades too early, losing all your profits by chasing the markets to catch that last little move.

If the market could be predicted to behave in a certain way then there would be no need for books, videos, and seminars about trading. We would be better off learning how to read tarot cards or astrological charts. The markets are really a microcosm of human psychology coupled with a dose of insider trading.

With the limited knowledge afforded to the retail trader, it is difficult to pick absolute tops and absolute bottoms. By attempting to trade within these parameters there is a significant need for risk management as opposed to money management in order to protect yourself from the unknown.

The weakness of the majority of swing trading is the belief that stop losses or risking only 2 percent is sufficient risk management. This could not be further from the truth.

While less demanding in actual face time in front of the trading screen, swing trading requires a lot of preparation time to determine entry, profit, and loss exits. This preparation time is essential in order to set a trade and forget it. A lack of preparation time along with an insufficient risk plan leads many swing traders to give up.

Position Trader

A position trader (trend trader) is defined as "a trader who attempts to capture gains through the analysis of an asset's momentum in a particular direction." What these position traders are looking to do is to make the big bucks, no matter what the day-to-day fluctuations may be.

This is similar to buying and holding stocks. The belief is that there are only two ways to make money in the markets: either you can afford to make quick sniper attacks or you catch a trend at its beginning and hold on.

There is sound logic in wanting to be a position trader, particularly in the current commodity bull market. The euro has increased from 89 cents to breaking over $1.50. If you had traded a euro futures contract you would have made $76,250; if you had held onto a euro spot trade you would have made $61,000.

The same thing has happened with crude oil. Crude oil,, has gone from a price of $12/barrel to breaking over $100/barrel. A position trader that caught that entire move would have made $88,000.

Position trading can have great rewards, as the above examples can attest to. The core problem with position trading is that only with 20/20 hindsight can we see the actual result of buying and holding.

During the wild fluctuations of the markets' movements it becomes difficult to maintain a conviction. Long or short, position trading can be unnerving at times.

Rarely does a market simply move straight up or straight down. The peaks and valleys along the way give the illusion that a trend has stopped or a move is reversing itself, only to have it resume unexpectedly.

While on the surface these moves may not amount to much more than a few percentage points here and there, the margin leverage makes it difficult to hold onto trades for the long haul. For example, if you trade a market with a 10 to 1 leverage, a 4 percent move against you is the equivalent of a 40 percent loss.

What trader would willingly give up 40 percent gains in order to make just 10 percent? None in their right mind, but that is what is asked of the position trader time and time again.

By not knowing if the particular market they are trading has reached its plateau, a position trader must be willing to give up what he has for the possibility of gaining more. This simple fact makes it difficult for small retail traders to be both psychologically and financially prepared to properly hold onto trades for the long haul, even if they know that the market will continue in the direction they expect.

Chapter 2

Various Ways of Trading Like a Pro

There are various ways you can learn how to trade stocks. Here are the some of the best ways that you can learn to trade stocks online quickly.

1. Read a bunch of trading books - If you are interested in long term investing where you buy a stock and hold for a few years, then look for books on the topic of fundamental analysis.

If you are the type of person who are impatient for holding stocks for that long, then short term trading might be your style. If that's the case, pick up some books about technical analysis and you will learn how to read a stock chart and swing trade stocks.

2. Register for online course - This is much more expensive than reading books on your own because you will have to pay for coaches and the online courses. You can do a Google search for free online courses and pick up some good resources.

However, those free stock courses generally give you a quick introduction to the stock market and then if you want to learn more, you will end up paying for an expensive price.

3. eBooks - This is one of the easiest and cheapest way to get you started in the trading stocks because there are some sites that offers you free stock training eBooks on both technical analysis and fundamental analysis. Just try to get all of them and paper trade their system and see how the trading strategies work for you.

4. Stock forums - Another way to learn about stock trading is to participate in stock forums and asking questions. You can actually learn from other members in the forum. However, this will take a significant amount of time and patience from you to digest everything.

5. Stock trading blogs - There are free blogs out there that can teach you about stock trading. Try to follow a couple of these stock blogs and see how the owner is trading. You can often learn some pretty good trading strategies from them that may actually work for you.

6. Paper trade - No matter which method you use to learn trading, you must spend at least 2-3 months paper trading. This way you won't risk any money as a stock market beginner.

There is really no magic in trading the stock market, you will really need to constantly educate yourself and learn new methods or trading strategies on a day to day basis. The good thing about trading is it is actually not that hard.

Once you get the balls rolling, you can quickly learn new trading ideas and systems that you can make money with.

My advice to everyone who is interested in trading is to keep a trading journal on every stock you buy and sell. This way you will learn from mistakes and improve your trading skills in the long term. You will also have to learn how to exercise discipline as that's the key to successful trading.

Let me go into the various winning strategies that can make you a pro in the stock market world.

Chapter 3

Momentum Trading Strategy

Momentum day trading can be extremely profitable when done correctly.

Day trading momentum stocks can be a very risky adventure. You can lose a lot of money when you pick the wrong opportunities.

The stockmarket can present you with a lot of hot stocks every day. Some of them are extremely risky while others are not as good as they seem. When you know how to identify and approach the best momentum stock opportuntites, you are able to generate a consistent and respectable amount of money in a very short period of time.

We know that day trading stocks with momentum is not the only way to make money investing online in stock market. But it can be the fastest way when you do it right.

We also understand that a lot of people shy away from momentum stocktrading and think that only a few online stock traders can profit from it. It's true. Only those traders with proven knowledge have the ability to profit consistently from momentum stocks.

You don't necessarily have to trade momentum hot stocks all the time. But you can learn how to take advantage of them when you encounter the best stock opportunities while at the same time limiting your trading risk.

Chapter 4

Sound Education in Stock Strategy

A very important technique when engaging in stock trading is to get sufficient education not only on how to trade with stocks, but also about the different market movements, what factors can affect the market and your chosen stocks, and so on.

Playing the stock market based only on speculation and guesses is definitely a huge no-no. All newbie traders should not skip on this vital stock investment advice of learning everything there is about stocks, the market, and, of course, must-use stock trading strategies.

Although some may say that others have the knack for trading, one's success mainly depends on one's knowledge, skills, and expertise. If you want to learn to trade stocks, there are now so many options available to help you gain mastery of this numbers game.

Fortunately, current technological developments have made it possible even for laymen to become expert traders. Here are four ways to help you become an expert trader.

In trading, the importance of having basic stock market education can never be emphasized enough.

Given that stock market trading has its own jargon and is based on some complex principles known only those who understand them, enrolling in a stock trading course is actually one of the best related investments you can make.

Just like any other introductory course, these kinds of classes teach you basic concepts in trading and the common strategies utilized; these classes can also help you gain familiarity with daily trading practices.

Moreover, some courses even offer extra services. All you need to do is set aside some time and money as you choose the right "teacher" that can satisfy your needs.

Master the Basic Strategies

As you progress through the course, you will encounter terms, such as "swing trading," "trending," or "day trading," to name a few. These refer to the basic strategies utilized by traders from all over the world.

Depending on the market and price movements you are following, the application of the proper strategy could yield handsome dividends for the trader. Accordingly, the improper application could lead to disastrous results.

Thus, apart from acquiring basic stock market education, it is important for an aspiring trader to master these strategies as well.

Practice Through Paper Trading

If you really want to learn to trade stocks, then you must be willing to invest time and money in this activity. However, you must do so with utmost care, which is why before you engage in actual trading, it is better that you first try out simulated trading or paper trading.

Some internet-based companies offer service though which you can open a practice trading account and you can "trade" without using actual money. This way, you can practice without the actual risks involved. The more you practice, the better you get. Thus, it is not a bad idea to try and practice first before engaging in actual trading.

Subscribe to a Daily Stock Report Service

There are so many tools that you can now use to help you become an expert trader. For instance, companies nowadays offer to provide stock reports and stock picks delivered to you on a regular basis prior to each trading day.

As you learn to trade stocks, you will soon find out how very useful these tools are in formulating the right strategies to help you generate the most profits.

Chapter 5

Create an Account with a Reputable Stock Company Over the Web

Included in the list of stock trading strategies is for you to set up an account with a reputable or trusted stock company over the internet. You need an online account so you can start to trade with stocks.

Before signing up with any stock-company, however, check on its feedback, reviews, and reputation, as it is important that you own an account with a stocks company that can really give you good service.

Remember that online stock companies are where you can receive tools for analysis of your trades, stock charts, and so on, thus, a stock investment advice you should not forget is to carefully choose your stock-company.

You should never, ever trade with stocks without even completely understanding the techniques and strategies. Keep in mind that you need these advices and information in order to up the chances of you making stock-trades that bring about a lot of earnings that happen more often, or consistently.

Chapter 6

CFD Trading Strategy

CFD trading strategy is different from the strategies offered by other brokers. CFD stands for Contracts for Difference Trading. One of the most famous trading strategies among the various CFD trading strategies is pair trading.

Pair trading is famous for low risk and high probability gains. This technique is an arbitrage technique, which means balancing a long trade versus a short trade. Pair trading allows traders to diversify the risk.

By pair trading, a trader can reduce the exposure as the big market moves. In this strategy, a small trader will trade in unchanged sector but a trader with high-risk capacity will make aggressive pair trades like pairing up in different sectors or even on different exchanges.

Most of the people enter into share trading without any knowledge and these people trade on those tips, which are based on rumors. This strategy leads them to short-term profit but it can generate heavy losses in long run. Therefore, proper knowledge is necessary to move ahead in trading business.

CFD trading tips are being provided by brokers and experts to help the traders in trading. The first tip for CFD traders is to gain knowledge about the business policies and then take a next step. Second tip is not to trade more than they can afford.

One should not hold the loss shares and should not predict that it will rise in future. They should also quit the share investment as soon as it moves up from certain level. Prediction will only lead to losses.

One should only think about the long-term gains, if one is betting in short term then that might make profit in pennies, so try to deal in long term. While trading, the trader should not panic and should not make hasty decisions, as that will lead them to lose. These were some of the strategies or tips to help people in trading.

If one is trading on CFD then he/she will definitely have a CFD spreadsheet log, which is an EXCEL based spreadsheet. These spreadsheets track all of the relevant trading data according to the trader's individually customized needs.

These spreadsheets make the management of CFD business easier. The spreadsheet holds the trading log of daily transactions and provides a calculator to calculate the average price and quantity to know the profit/loss at the end of the day.

Chapter 7

Options as a Conservative Trading Strategy

Prior to analyzing our strategies we require a means of evaluating the quality of a strategy. Profit Factor is generally used by analysts to determine which trading strategies have the best reward to risk ratios.

It requires a record of trades to calculate. Profit Factor [PF] is the sum of the winning trades divided by the sum of the losing trades:

PF = £ Winning Trades / £ Losing Trades

For example, PF = 3 would imply each dollar risked would result in three dollars reward. Obviously, the higher PF, the better.

Successive Losing Trades

Profit Factor, by itself, is not adequate to judge better strategies. The market is always changing. One sector, such as semiconductors, might be hot for a time and cool during another; value stocks have had their moments of favor; even internet stocks without any tangible assets have had their bubble.

We need to be prepared for the likeliness of successive losing trades. Not only are successive losing trades damaging to resources, but they are also debilitating emotionally and can inhibit our will to follow our strategy.

A Stock Trading Strategy - Rooster Tail

For this article let us consider a proprietary strategy called Rooster Tail. It trades five stocks with a market timer (SPXTimer from October 2006 to September 2010 only in bull markets). In addition to the timer, exits are controlled via gain and loss stops.

The initial investment was $100,000 or $20,000 per position. Profits are reinvested.

As you can see, its back-trading statistics are very good:

Profit Factor	:	2.8
Successive losing trades	:	6
Gain	:	218.21% [$100,000 ¨ $313,212]
Annual Rate of Return	:	56.29%
% Wining Trades	:	62.23%

Rooster Tail Traded With Options

Options are strange beasts that have many interesting properties. Often it is possible to buy an option for less than 10% of the price of the stock. This is an important association. Were we willing to trade the stock with a 10% stop it would mean risking at least a 10% loss.

On the other hand, using the option in lieu of the stock limits the loss to at at most 10% - it cannot be more than that. As you can see, options offer the opportunity to gain more and lose less than if you just purchased the stock. Employing options this way eliminates the need for stops.

Options, also, reward wins better than it penalizes losses. For example, if we compare a stock gain versus an equivalent loss, we would expect the corresponding option dollar gain to be greater than the loss. This is because the option loss can be no more than its cost. Like a stock, the upward potential for an option is unlimited.

As a result, if at least 50% of your stock trades would be winners, the options would present a huge advantage. Why? Because your gains would be much greater with options and the losses would be less. Furthermore, if the average win greater than the average stock loss it would further improve the odds.

Stops are often recommended as a tool for managing risk. They are insufficient. See 'Is it Possible to Invest Profitably Without Stops?'. This strategy does not employ stops.

In our simulation, each trade of Rooster Tail is replaced with an option trade of the stocks. The options were entered at the same time the stock was bought and exited at the same time as the stock was sold.

The strike price was the stock price rounded up to the next dollar; initial duration was 60 days unless the stock trade was longer - then it was 90 days; volatility was a fixed 35%.

We want to limit the investment allocation to the options portion of our portfolio to 10% of the bank. Therefore, the initial option allocation was $10,000 or $2,000 per position. Profits and losses are applied to the bank. All investments were for a fixed amount during a signal.

The statistics with options are even better:

Profit Factor	:	3.4
Successive losing trades	:	6
Gain	:	273.71% [$100,000 ¨ $373,707]
Annual Rate of Return	:	70.6%
% Wining Trades	:	56.8%

If used properly, options can be traded profitably as a conservative investment strategy. With this strategy, 90% of your capital always remains in cash. This is the ultimate hedge against successive losing trades.

Stocks cannot match this strategy in terms of Profit Factor, Annual Rate of Return or safety. Furthermore, this option strategy can be employed in IRAs

Chapter 8

Gap Trading Strategy

You can search the internet, or go to your local library, and find a plethora of information on complicated, hard to understand, currency trading strategies.

Though forex education is important, there are many simple, time-tested forex trading strategies that can be used immediately and give you profitable results. Profits are, as we all know, the bottom line.

Profiting from Gap Trading

Gap trading is not a new strategy. It's been used in all investment markets for a very long time. To learn this forex trading technique is relatively easy. Gap trading in an attempt to take advantage of the difference, or "gap," in price between the close of the previous day with the open of the following day.

If the open price is above the previous day's close, this is commonly referred to as "gapping up". If the open price is below the previous day's close price, this is called "gapping down". If the open is at the same price level, then there was no gap.

Forex Trading and Gaps

Generally, in forex trading this strategy tends to be ignored; most people feel that as currencies are traded 24 hours a day, there is no true opening or closing prices. That being said, some people maintain that gap trading in forex trading can be successful 85% of the time.

If this is the case, there is money to be made. The question becomes: How can you trade gaps in the forex market?"

If you ignore the 24-hour time frame associated with forex trading, and set up an opening and closing time to create an artificial market, you can provide yourself with an open high low close data range. Based on that data range, you would be able to trade gaps. Another forex trading strategy is basically to ignore trading on Saturday and Sunday, when volume is thin and most of the world is not working. Under this scenario, you establish a closing time on Friday and an opening time on Monday. Based on the gap, you take the appropriate position.

Unlike what you might think, the forex currency trading strategy for gaps is contrary by nature. That is to say, you do the opposite of what's intuitive. If the price gaps up, you sell. If the price gaps down, you buy.

This forex currency trading strategy works more often than not, and thus, it's a simple process that can generate great profits.

Chapter 9

Leverage Strategy

One of the most successful and well-known forex trading strategies is leverage. A strategy based on leverage, allows you to make hundred or even thousand times the amount of money you have in your Forex account for trading. It's a great strategy if you can master it.

There are many success stories from forex traders who have used the leverage strategy to make record breaking profits. But before you start applying this strategy, you will need to learn as much as you can about the forex market, and what and how effects the prices to rise and fall.

The misuse of leverage is the magical force that is misunderstood. The majority of stock traders believe that they have to use the 20-to-1 leverage of futures or the 500-to-1 leverage of forex in order to trade them, and that is not the case. Futures and forex can be traded just like stocks.

The face value of a euro contract, U.S. $152,000 as of this writing, can be invested in euros and an investor can make or lose money in a EUR/US contract with a lot less volatility. The same can be said of a gold futures contract.

The face value of a gold contract is $92,000. An investor can put up the entire $92,000, eliminating his leverage risk, and just gain or lose on the true value of gold going up or down.

Because leverage is the key factor that separates futures and forex trading from stock investing, it stands to reason that the majority of the other factors will remain the same, such as the daisy chain effect and the strategies to exploit it.

There are stocks, CFDs, single stock futures, and options, each one designed to protect the other. If you are holding on to a long stock position, like 97 percent of all stock traders, then you can protect yourself from a downturn in the stock with a CFD or a single stock futures position.

If you are in a CFD or a single stock futures position, you could use either of these instruments to protect each other or use a stock option to protect the CFD, single stock future, or stock position. The mechanics are identical to the futures and forex market.

Chapter 10

Stop-loss Order Forex Trading Strategy

Stop-loss order is another great strategy for forex trading. Stop-loss order strategy works simply by identifying a point where you will not trade. Meaning it will identify this point before you begin the trading.

Be careful when using this strategy. Make sure you are able to analyze trading signals, and avoid mistakes in prediction. Making a mistake in predicting forex market, no matter how small, could cost you dearly. So, make decisions wisely

A stop-loss strategy revolves around placing an order with a broker, or an online stock broker, to minimize the loss on a security position. Also known as a stop order or stop-market order, a stop-loss order allows the investor to determine their loss limit in advance.

You can either buy or sell a certain stock when a specified price is reached. Then when that specific price is reached, the stop-loss order is entered as a market order, allowing the broker to buy or sell the stock at the current market price.

For example, a stop-loss order of 10% below the stock price will limit the loss to 10%. Of course, the stop-loss order is a fail-safe although it is not completely accurate. A fast moving market may result in a slightly higher or lower stock price sale or purchase.

What are the pros and cons of using the stop-loss strategy for stock trading? The advantage of having a stop-loss order in place will allow investors to focus on other issues, rather than the constant, daily monitoring of a stock's performance in a stock market.

This small but important factor clears up a lot of room, especially if you are worried about taking big losses. The disadvantage of this order is that simple daily market fluctuations for a stock can trigger the stop-loss, pushing you out of an otherwise good position.

Most savvy investors have different views on stop-loss orders. However, this strategy depends on what kind of investor you are. If your portfolio is well diversified with hundreds of positions, losses on a few specific positions may not matter as much. But if you're a single investor with a few positions, it could be a crucial step to protecting your capital.

Stop-loss orders are especially important for trend-following strategies. A large loss with a trend strategy could signify that the original entry signal has turned. A stop-loss order would minimize severe losses and preserve the investor's capital.

The overall benefit of a stop-loss order in most cases will outweigh the negatives. Since there are no costs, except for the commission when the buy or sell is issued, a stop-loss order essentially acts as an insurance against the opposite direction.

Keeping in mind that stop-loss orders cannot be used for certain securities like penny stocks, picking a stop-loss percentage that allows for daily stock price fluctuations while preventing the most downside risk is a strong insurance policy that can protect your capital and profit with the upside.

Chapter 11

Automated Forex Trading System

Automated forex trading is the favorite forex trading system of many successful traders. It makes trading Forex a whole a lot easier, by automatically determining when to enter a trad, or when to exit one.

Of course, the price and the point where the program would enter or exit a trade is predetermined. Automated forex trading has its own risks as well, but the rewards are far greater that the risks.

There are many great automated forex trading system for a reasonable price, that will make trading in Forex market joyful. And if you use the right automated forex trading system, you can make unbelievable profits.

There are many software out there that can automated your tradings for you, but one of the newer ones that have generated quite a buzz recently is Forex Neutrino. It's a little costly (about $100), but if you are a serious investor, it's worth it.

These forex trading strategies can give you much better trade opportunities in the forex market. But remember, no matter what system or strategy you use, there is no guarantee for succeeding.

You need to keep in mind that no strategy alone is going to give you the perfect trading system. These strategies are here to help you maximize your success rate while minimizing your risks. Testing and constantly adapting your strategies for the better, will ensure your success in making money with Forex trading.

Automated forex trading strategies are required for you to be profitable in the already complicated foreign exchange market. The foreign exchange market is a trillion dollar trade involving millions of traders and speculators all over the world.

It is not only a place for all winners to multiply their earnings from their original investment amount, but also a place where the losers are making the attempts to obtain back what they have lost, or lose even more. If you are planning to venture into the foreign exchange business, the easiest way to succeed is duplicating the proven techniques practiced by the successful traders.

With years of experience under their belt, the pros will be able to tell you which systems will make you lose your investments and which ones will make you rich. These techniques separate the forex champions from the losers.

To prevent you from falling into these group of losers, this chapter will elaborate one of the easy forex trading strategies that had generated truckloads of money to the majority of professional traders out there.

It is even easy enough for new traders to practice and has proven its worthiness in the forex game field: automated forex systems or forex trading robots

Forex trading robots are basically software systems that have been programmed by a team of computer programmers in collaboration with forex professional players.

The robot is able to extract real-time key investment data, converts them by using the algorithms in the programming codes into quality analysis and create vital reports to aid in your decision to speculate among the many currencies, including to buy or sell in perfect timing.

However, the quality of analysis and reports generated by the robot is very much dependent on the capabilities of the programmers, and much more of the forex guy. The more experienced the forex guy is, the more reliable the robot.

With good input, the programmers will be able to conduct the precise and required programming codes to ensure that robot fulfills the trading necessities, in order for you to make profits, instead of making loses while trading.

Here are some tips for choosing the best automated forex trading robots:

1. Crisis proof. Choose a robot which is capable of re-adjusting to the changing market conditions. Should the market suddenly become too volatile (and therefore, too risky to trade), the volatility filter of the robot must be able to intervene and take the robot to an early exit.

The bot must also able to adjust automatically to the conditions of a specific brokerage in addition to being compatible with both the instant execution brokers and the market execution ones. These features could only be experienced after you purchase the robots. Most vendors will provide you a refund should you are not satisfied with the robot.

2. Low initial investment requirement. Choose a robot which requires a minimum of $450 for you to start trading on EUR/USD. Only if you wish to trade on both EUR/USD and USD/JPY, then you need to have a minimum of $4,000 in the trading account.

Since most profits are generated on EUR/USD, so a minimum of $450 will be perfectly sufficient. It is important to note that if a robot programmer tells you that you can trade a forex robot with $100 or even $50, he is actually after your hard-earned money.

Of course, you CAN technically trade even with as low as $1.00, but it will result in an instant margin call and put you out of business faster than you can hit the stop trading button. $450 here means that you can safely increase your capital and that all security filters have enough room to kick into action to preserve your money and your gains.

3. Easy setup. Find a robot which is easy to utilize, like a "set and forget" robot. Indicators include the

requirements of not having to enter complex lists of settings, to upload files into various folders and to watch the robot during its trading. Everything should already be done for you.

4. No liquidity issues. The best robot must trade DURING the market hours and not between them, unlike many other unreliable forex robots. This aspect ensures sufficient liquidity at all times, no matter what the situation on the market is and how many people are using the robot. The liquidity during the forex market hours totals in the trillions of dollars. Therefore, even if we had millions of people using the bot at the same time, it would not affect the currency market in any way.

6. Careful and safe trading environment. The perfect robot will trade during the different opening and closing times of stock exchanges in different parts of the world. That way, we will always be overall in profit no matter what the current situation is on the market.

The robot's time of market entry needs to be at a fixed time of the day, during which the massive asset transfer from US stock exchanges to the European ones takes place.

The American trading floors (NYSE, CBOT, etc.) close down for the night when the European ones (Frankfurt, Amsterdam, Brussels etc.) are about to open in the morning, therefore boosting up the demand for the Euro against the US Dollar, as all stocks in the US are being traded in US Dollars and all stocks in Europe are being traded in Euros.

The same is true for the USD/JPY currency pair- when the Japanese stock trading (where all stocks are traded for the Yen) ceases in the evening (NIPPON, NIKKEI etc.), the American one is about to resume in the morning.

7. Flexible trading. The robot must be able to trade in the two popular majors - EUR/USD and USD/JPY - which are offered by pretty much every broker in the market. Moreover, the spreads on these two pairs (mainly because of their

popularity) are marginally low, which further serves to your advantage.

8. Auto adjusting to evade errors. If a news release suddenly hits the market and a broker drastically increases its spread in response, your robot must be able to recognize it and automatically cuts the starting lot size for its trading cycles and once the spread is back to normal, trading with the standard starting lot size resumes.

This aspect prevents the robot from being unable to close the cycle of time because of the suddenly increased spread. If your computer, VPS or internet connection experiences an outage, the robot must be able to be restarted from a different computer.

It needs to be able to recognize the trades it opened from the old computer as part of its trading cycle and will proceed with the trading as if nothing has happened.

Why are automated trading strategies becoming so popular?

I believe that in order to judge the true efficiency and performance of a trading system, one need to trade every set up that it offers, not just the ones that occur when you happen to be at your trading desk.

If you apply an automated trading system to your trading you will be able to accurately assess your system to determine its effectiveness. Trading programs are a very effective means of eliminating errors and emotions from your Forex trading. For this reason alone, many discretionary traders moved over to automated trading programs.

Automated trading strategies are becoming increasingly popular amongst private individual forex traders. In a recent study conducted (by IBFX) 94% of traders said that they would use the same or increase the amount of automated trading they will perform in the next twelve months.

Only 6% stated that they would decrease their use of automated trading strategies. On top of that the study also showed that as of September 2010, 56%

of all trading activity on the New York Stock Exchange was high frequency, or computer automated trading.

In 2004 algorithmic trading made up a mere 4% of total forex trading. By 2007 this figure had risen to 28% and estimates are that currently around 50% of all forex trades are automated and these figures are expected to continue to climb rapidly. There is no doubt that automated forex trading systems are gaining in popularity.

The main reason for this growth in automated trading is technology. As technology is a driving force in most other fast moving sectors, so it has had a huge impact on forex trading systems?

The first major step towards the development of auto trading systems was the move away from floor trading to computerised trading. Once this occurred trading firms developed their own trading systems to place orders through the new electronic exchanges.

Retail traders now have access to technology that previously was only available to these large banks and institutional trading desks. With the highly advanced trading platforms now available to individual forex traders around the globe, they can now compete on an equal footing. As traders began to implement automation in their Forex day trading systems they soon realised the huge opportunities that they presented. Traders began to share ideas and approaches and now automation is the way of the future for individual traders.

Automated strategies will improve your performance as your auto system is able to follow more markets, more efficiently, more of the time. Manual trading is limited to the number of hours you can stay focussed in a trading day. Realising this, many long time manual traders have moved over to Forex auto trading programs.

Automated trading systems are so much more efficient as they require less human intervention and therefore less cost. Traders may only have a few hours to spend on their trading each.

An auto trading system will allow part-time traders to trade full time by trading the market on their behalf. Traders then just need to monitor their systems performance. Day traders are now able to focus more on research, system improvements and keeping up with market trends rather than sitting in front of their trading screen waiting for the next set up.

This serves to improve their overall performance by focusing on important issues, not merely the mundane tasks.

Chapter 12

Online Forex Trading Strategies

Now that there are hundreds of forex margin brokers, millions of free forex trading tips websites and literally hundreds of thousands of forex day trading strategy "home based business" forex traders, we can say that virtually anyone with an internet connection can trade forex with the pros.

In any power trading strategy, a proven trading method will mean that through Forex strategy testing and by using trading risk management, no more than one or two per cent of a total account value is put at risk in a single trade.

This is key in the path to big forex profits. Any trader beginning out will look at the trading methodologies available to them and decide to create trading rules for their forex trading strategy.

Forex trading (currency trading) beginners should be aware therefore not only of technical and fundamental analysis and predicting forex prices, but also of how to be a trading strategy tester and to have strong forex trading rules that help them to make the big forex profits they are seeking.

The alternative is to have more experienced forex trading systems used by more experienced traders end up causing you to lose all your money in your forex business - the harshest possible outcome.

Having the following in place could assist you in getting started right away in forex trading (currency trading): a forex trading software platform; a free forex trading strategy (or a paid for one for that matter); an understanding of fundamental and technical analysis and a trading risk management system.

From these elements (and also the support of a daily forex strategy briefing from a margin broker or some other site) you can start forex trading with your own forex trading strategy rules.

Learning currency trading online needs to begin with sound trading risk management and how to manage your trading account balance by making intelligent risk decisions with your trading account. The risks can be higher with forex because the moves in a week can be equivalent to a month in stock moves. Volatility is to be expected.

Forex strategy testing can either be done through using a practice account through your broker or by paper trading your strategy. A third option is to use software such as Forex Strategy Tester which can run a simulation of what could happen if you trade by your rules with some limitations on accuracy.

As mentioned, free forex trading strategy tips are available all over the web. The truth is that the Forex trading market needs to be treated as a business that runs like a forex trading machine as much as possible. This is key if you are to make big forex profits in live trading.

Lack of regulation means that anyone can sell a "scalping trading strategy" or so-called "foolproof trading method" and make themselves out to be an expert or even say they are a long term bank trader when they are not.

There is a need for caution therefore when deciding on where to get your forex education because not any Forex trading guide is actually going to help in your predicting Forex prices in the near, medium or long terms.

It behooves you to go out and look at what is on offer from Forex trading websites and learn more about the global currency markets after you have read this article. Some sites are listed in the resource box at the end to start you off. Trading forex online then presents challenges.

The rest of this article will address those challenges. In order to trade effectively, a forex trading guide is needed for the initiate in to the

Forex markets to be able to learn online currency trading, understand trading risk management and how to manage money, discover technical and fundamental analysis, how these types of analysis of the market differ and how to apply them in creating a Forex trading machine.

This means that after all the cogs are set in place you will have a forex trading machine that enables you to its like a professional and make decisions based in the moment and on the facts that are presented to you, rather than guess or gambling work - although there is invariably an element of risk, your job is to eliminate the risk as much as possible in applying your trading strategy.

To make this happen, you will start to think about what you may need in order to implement your trading strategy. For example, will you be needing a daily forex strategy briefing from either a paid service or a free provider of its strategy briefings -

such as perhaps your broker or a third party service.

In your technical analysis will you be utilising traditional indicators such as those involved in a bands trading strategy (Bollinger Bands), will you rely on charts created by a its platform or other currency price forecast type service or will you be professional analyst charts to make your decisions?

A proven trading method is hard to come by. There are educators who have been trading Forex for banks and other institutions for many years.

However they are still going to find it incredibly difficult to pass on their years of knowledge, at least not in the time most people want to go from knowing nothing about forex trading (currency trading) to being an expert and making money with its as a business.

In sum, it is multidimensional. There are several aspects of absolute importance. These include strategy, both in terms of trading and money management, education - both initial and ongoing and focusing in on mastering a specific area whether that be a particular currency pair or aspect within the field - such as global economics of a particular country.

Chapter 13

Understanding the Trading Halts Day Trading Strategy

The "trading halt strategy" is a day trading strategy that is used to indicate a buy long or sell short signal for investment opportunities that can take advantage of the substantial increase in volume.

The "trading halt strategy" is a day trading strategy that is used to indicate a buy long or sell short signal for investment opportunities that can take advantage of the substantial increase in volume and volatility of stocks with pending material news to generate extraordinary returns.

Day traders may place side bets as part of their trading strategies, using options to try to make quick gains on short term movements of a stock while the market tries to determine the long term trends of stock.

For example, it is common that a material event may lead to a trading halt in stock. Most of the time the event is already announced by a company but the outcome whether positive or negative is not known.

This occurs in biotechnology regularly where a company has completed a drug trial and is about to announce the results. It also occurs in the mergers and acquisition arena where there is a rumor that a company is in play to be acquired but prior to the announcement of an agreement to be acquired the stock of the company is halted.

The stock of the company is halted prior to the announcement of the material news by the stock exchange in order to maintain a 'fair' and orderly trading market in the stock.

If the event has been pre-announced by a company then prior to that announcement that leads to a stock halt, day traders are in the market taking positions based on the expectation of a favorable or unfavorable outcome of the event.

This is a short term event that usually leads to a significant increase in the volatility of the stock. The day trader's goal is to turn a quick profit shortly after the announcement. Timing is essential so it is critical to find out what stocks are halted and why so a day trader can determine if there is an opportunity to make a quick profit after the stock trading halt is lifted.

What the traders are typically counting on is that the market will over react one way or they other depending on the outcome of the event that is disclosed after the trading halt.

Since the market tends to over react to news, this means that prior to the results being announced there should be a short term spike or decline in the stock price with significantly increased liquidity in the market for the stock.

Very shortly after the spike or decline, the trader will unwind their position at a profit. Since there is substantial liquidity because there are many people trade on the news, there is an opportunity to take significant positions without the concern that they will not be able to exit those positions or that the exit of position in the stock will affect the stock price.

There are several services that may assist a day trader in finding these opportunities. Some are paid services and some are free service with realtime or near real-time email or text message announcements of stocks that have become halted.

As a day trader, the key task is getting in the position take advantage of the stock trading halts. Clearly some research and guts are necessary to take a bet on material non-public news before it is announced.

Chapter 14

Currency Strategies

The forex market is rapidly becoming one of the most popular places to make money, and forex trading and currency strategies are an important part of being a successful trader.

Reading a trading guide online is a great place to start, however there are some important things about the foreign exchange market that set it apart from other similar trading centers.

Perhaps the most remarkable thing about the foreign exchange is the extremely high liquidity. This means that the goods traded on the market, in this case currency, do not change in value when they are converted to other goods.

This high liquidity makes for low market power across the board. Market power refers to the ability of a single entity to raise or lower forex trading prices, and a low overall market power means a high level of competition.

This near-perfect competition makes the playing field even between huge corporations and individual investors, and is a great place to invest if you are doing so on your own with a limited amount of funds.

Reading up on currency strategies or a trading guide online makes it even easier to get ahead, so that individuals can actually beat out corporate investors with the right amount of research.

Currency strategies and trading guides are, essentially, ways to invest money that use predictions about the future of various economies based on world events. For example, say you know that a new oil field was recently discovered in a country that has a relatively low amount of exported oil.

This oil field, if significant enough, could drastically alter that country's economy, and therefore the value of its money. A trading guide online or currency strategy could help you take advantage of this, and are also designed to make trading easier and faster.

Forex trading is not as difficult as some people believe, and currency strategies are designed to make it even easier.

A trading guide online can also be a huge help, so whether you're a new investor looking for an exciting, profitable new market to dive into, or an experienced trader who only needs a little extra help succeeding, consider checking out the numerous trade strategies available across the web.

Chapter 15

Good Foreign Exchange Strategy

Good foreign exchange trading strategies can take you a far way in the forex market and put you well ahead of other traders. First in opening with foreign exchange trading strategies.

Good foreign exchange trading strategies can take you a far way in the forex market and put you well ahead of other traders.

First in opening with foreign exchange trading strategies, you've got to understand simple but important aspects of trading such as the foreign exchange trading spreads.

This is the difference between the ask price and the bid price, or in other terms the point which you buy to the buy which you sell. This is recorded in pips and you obviously want to maximize your pips just like the stock market by getting in low and getting out high.

Many traders turn to practice accounts to hone their foreign exchange trading strategies in before committing to the real market.

The only difference is what you invest with as virtual currency is the focus in practice trading so that you can trade your gains and losses accordingly without any real financial risk to yourself.

Another more up and coming of the best foreign exchange trading strategies entails relying heavily on a forex program. There are two significant types of programs for different foreign exchange trading strategies.

First, fully automated programs exist which act as robots which place and end trades for you in the forex market. They require 24 hour internet access to real time market data to find high probability trading opportunities and invest in them accordingly.

Once they find a trading opportunity which they deem as being low risk, they invest accordingly with whatever capital you give it. The program then tracks that trade's performance, ensuring you are constantly earning on it and the trend continues. Once it reverses out of your favor, it trades the now bad investment away, thus shielding you from debt and loss.

These programs are more ideal for first time traders and those without a great deal of time or experience because it takes trading completely out of your hands.

The other major type of forex program for foreign exchange trading strategies is the signal generator. This is essentially a program which acts like stock picker but for the forex world.

It keeps constant tabs on real time market behavior 24 hours a day just like the automated trading program to find high probability and reliable trends, but they won't invest for you.

Instead, this program generates and sends the pick to you so that you can trade accordingly. This obviously requires more know how and experience of being able to enact your own trades and is for traders who want more control over their trading.

Chapter 16

Binary Betting Trading Strategy

This method can be used anytime during the binary. Is the binary bet value oscillating more than the spread? For what it's worth here are the three techniques that made profits in the trading binary bets.

Binary Betting Strategies: Method 1

Q. This method can be used anytime during the binary. Is the binary bet value oscillating more than the spread? If so, AND you're in a generally surging market (observed from previous binaries, and the news), buy as low as you can and then sell AS SOON as the binary has flipped you into profit.

It doesn't matter if you reach the maximum you could possibly obtain. With this technique, just take any profit - you will see one at some point during this 'random' period. By buying low in a surging market, ON AVERAGE, the trend should be upwards. If the market is going downwards, just use the opposite binary (i.e. falling) and do the same.

Binary Betting Tactics: Method 2

I had to do this on a Wall Street binary, as Gold/Silver had closed. This might be more risky as it appeared more volatile. However, wait till about 2-5 minutes to go in the binary.

If the graph has been >50 for most of the hour AND it is now around 90 AND you are more than approximately 10 market points above the initial value then go in with your biggest amount and count down the seconds. This way you pretty much seem to be guaranteed ten times your stake. Anyhow, it worked the 3 times I did it.

Binary Betting System: Method 3

Other people - on more liquid/volatile markets (FTSE hourlies for example) betting on the reverse. Say the FTSE's already up 3% ten minutes into the hour and the binary's at 92/96.

You take it to fall (at 92). 45 minutes into the hour the FTSE has slipped back to only 2% up, and the binary's at 72/76. You can either close it out (and pocket 92-76 = 16pts profit) or hope it will drop further by the end, down to -0.1%, which would pocket you the whole 92pts as the binary would close at 0.

Thus the best way to profit from binaries appears to be to wait until about 3pm (London time): if the underlying Gold future had made a significant move in either direction (3-5pts) by then, and IG Index still had the binary valued around 80/85 (rising market) or 15/20 (falling) (because of the uncertainty), then it rarely reverses.

So you could get in at 85 and collect the 15pts change. Of course, this does depend on the 3pm-

and-significant-move trend coming off slightly more than 5 out of 6 days. This does *seem* to work pretty well - although days like yesterday would have had me crapping myself if I'd bought it to buy.

The last method is an interesting strategy because you're risking very little (in this example, only 8pts). During the hour there is often a recoil, and the binary dips a bit - so if you're watching it constantly you can cash in.

As far as I can tell however, it doesn't do a total reverse (i.e. a strong enough move to get the binary over 90 that then cancels) often enough at all times of the day - the index moves effectively randomly as it's the result of the movements of the 102 stocks on the FTSE. So leaving it hands-off until close you're on a loser.

Chapter 17

MACD as a Strategic Indicator in Stock Trading

MACD (Moving Average Convergence / Divergence). This indicator is basically a slightly more sophisticated moving average. Instead of measuring price data according to some arbitrary length, the MACD indicator takes the difference between 2 moving averages and then plots the changes graphically in bar chart form.

What you are left with is a sort of roller coaster effect which charts the ebbs and flows of price as it trends upward or downward.

MACD is an excellent trend indicator. Always begin with identifying the trend and then trade WITH it, never against it. Think of it as a one-way filter. If the MACD is sloping upward then only take long positions. Downward? Only take short positions.

If you like to trade on say the 5-minute chart, then go up a timeframe or two and compute the MACD for that chart. This is your guiding trend. Do not make the mistake of trying to trade off the MACD at the same 5-minute timeframe.

It will throw you off because you lack perspective. Always compute the trend off a higher (longer) timeframe (in this example the 10-minute or 15-minute chart). If you are a daily chart trader then use the trend off the weekly chart.

Chapter 18

Commodity Trading Strategy

What are Commodities?

Commodities are goods that are in broad demand and are pretty constant and do not differ much in terms of quality. For example, gold is gold whether it's mined in Africa or Australia.

Because of this standard in quality, these goods become useful tools for investment and trading. When you buy a barrel of crude oil for example, you know what you're getting and you won't get short-changed or cheated.

Examples of goods and products that can be traded as commodities include:

- ❖ Precious metals such as gold, silver and copper.
- ❖ Agricultural products such as rubber, corn, rice and sugar.
- ❖ Energy and industrial resources such as crude oil, coal and aluminum.
- ❖ Non-traditional "resources".
  Entrepreneurial people have started talking about "natural capital" and trading carbon emissions and weather.

Trading Commodities

When people talk about trading commodities, the majority of them are not actually buying one tonne of sugar and then selling it a week later.

Commodities are commonly traded using derivative tools such as futures. Buying a futures contract of an underlying commodity means you are buying the right to buy the commodity at a certain price at a certain future date.

In the meantime, the actual price of the commodity goes up and down from day to day.

This fluctuation makes the futures contract either go up or down in price depending on which direction the underlying commodity's price goes.

The Commodity Market

Commodities are traded internationally, and are traded on various exchanges around the world. Examples of these include the Chicago Mercantile Exchange, Australian Securities Exchange and the Tokyo Commodity Exchange.

These exchanges act as marketplaces where commodity futures contracts can be traded and exercised.

The prices of commodities rise and fall. Some are cyclical, while others depend on the current economic outlook and political circumstances. For example, the price of agricultural products like corn and rice fluctuates depending on the time of year, and also on the year's harvest.

On the other hand, commodities such as crude oil are very dependent on economic and political situations.

For example, if there's political instability such as war or government problems in the Middle East (where most of the oil producers are), the price of crude oil would rise. And the price would rise if the economy and industry are strong, and energy consumption is high; and vice versa.

Why Trade Commodities?

The cyclical and trending natures of commodities provide investors with the opportunity to trade in commodity futures. Investors are able to earn from trading commodity futures by being able to predict the cycles and profiting during economic and political upheavals.

Commodity futures can also be traded to hedge against the chance that the underlying commodity doesn't produce expected output in the current cycle.

Companies whose business involves those commodities would then hedge against that and earn some money from commodity futures even though their products don't sell well.

For investors and casual traders, commodity trading represents another method of trading other than shares or currency. The risks and rewards are similar, differentiated by the underlying commodities being traded.

If you are interested in commodity trading, you will need to do some research on the commodity you want to focus on, and analyse how its price varies depending on annual cycles as well and political and economic changes.

Chapter 19

Swing Trading Strategy

Most of the investors and the traders are well known about the Swing trading. If you are not among the day traders or long-term traders, then you fall in the list of swing traders. It says that you are holding the stock or a commodity for few days but not more than few weeks in every way.

This trading is believed to be a low risk speculation. When the swing patterns change due to certain fundamental impacts, then it may lead to a loss but you should not take it to heart so seriously because swing trading is not all about profits, there are chances of loss.

A Proper Look at Swing Trading Strategies:

It is a famous way of taking advantage on the short-term price versions of the stock market. It has got the reputation of high profile as it is a strong way to increase the benefits at the lowest risk value.

The best and excellent swing trading strategy requires the ability to select the stocks or the commodities that vacillates at the utmost ends. This strategy is enforced in a static market because the prices incline towards having minor versions on which the swing investor can take advantage.

In a stock market, where the rise is on constant flow or is in a constant downfall, swing strategy can't be enforced.

Why the newcomers choose the swing trading strategy?

They go for the swing trading strategy in the stock market because it owes lower risks and a shorter period of time involvement.

In order to attain higher benefits in a short term time period, the correct swing trading strategy has to be applied to trade in the stock market of the big companies. These stocks or commodities are known as large cap stocks which are popularly traded on most of the stock exchanges.

The large cap stocks shows higher amount of variations as compared to the other stocks or commodities. In this way you may get good profit experience in the trading.

What to Choose During the Swing Trading Strategy?

A swing trader should follow a certain stock for about few days when the price is in upwards direction. If the stock price gets into the opposite turn that is downward direction, then the trader should turns over to another stock that is on a high rise.

In order to have a successful swing trading, it is mandatory to choose a perfect and correct stock that constitutes an encouraging portion of stock market.

Besides the choice of stock or commodity, the selection of the market plays a vital role on deciding a perfect swing trading strategy. Whether the market is on rising trend or downfall trend, the stock prices usually move in one single direction. The variation is not so swinging.

The best strategy will be to hold on to the stocks for longer period of time. A swing trader will work at its best in a static market. The values of the stocks that are chief almost remain the same.

Chapter 20

Offshore Carry Trading Strategy

Carry trading is a type of investing in which people use the method of taking advantage of different rates in different currency markets and the strength of a particular currency to obtain loans in one currency to invest in a more profitable currency. It is commonly used in forex trading.

It can also be used in trading US currency when the difference between the US global credit interest rates and bond yields is significant enough to use to profit. People who use this technique with US currency are usually bond traders.

From the novice forex trader to the most seasoned investor of bonds, commodities, or currencies, the term Carry Trading has been widely known. It has first gained positive impact in the early 80's, but has acclaimed more popularly during the last decade among financiers and investors.

It is a very interesting and a popular trading strategy in the foreign market due to the monetary gains and profit that a trader gets, either with medium or long-term investments. But how is it done and what makes it work?

Carry Trade technically involves buying high interest currencies and then funding these by selling low interest currencies. In simple terms, it's just like borrowing money at say, 2% interest and then purchasing stocks or bonds with the same amount of money at say, 5% interest.

At the end of the year, the money grows by 3%, and all that will be your profit. Now, you might think the figures are small at an annual scenario... well, that might be true, but then again, think that the reason why carry trading gets all the hype is because we are talking daily returns here.

Imagine getting the results day in and day out. Pretty amazing, right? Knowing how the foreign financial tricks of the trade counts too. Traders make it a point to buy currencies from countries with high interest and a strong economy. That is to avoid fluctuating and dropping rates thereby messing up their investments.

Choosing the lower interest currency is also equally important. And in the usual currency pairs, the one on the low interest would be the Japanese Yen for its low borrowing cost.

Some of the more common pairs are: GBP/CHF, GBP/JPY, AEUR/JPY, CAD/JPY, and USD/JPY. Getting the best pair according to the current foreign currency exchange is key to making profit using the carry trade strategy.

Admittedly, the good profit returns experienced during 2000 - 2007 caved-in last 2008, depleting seven years worth of gains in just three months. The world has witnessed the economic slump and since then, forex traders have been keeping their fingers crossed things would carry trading pick up soon.

Three Must-know Golden Rules About Carry Trading

After implementing this strategy successfully many times over a large number of currencies, I would like to point out what I deem to be the 3 golden rules for forex carry trading.

1. Money management. I can summarize it a) only invest a small portion of your capital in any given trade, especially if you are just beginning and b) only trade with money you can afford to lose.

This is key in any trading strategy but even more in forex carry trading. This is because you will often be holding a carry position for reasonable amount of time, therefore over-investing or needing the money urgently for another reason (house repair) can cost you a large loss.

2. Always invest in developing your education and skills. Once again, important in any trading strategy but even more in forex carry trading. Carry trades imply holding positions in two different currencies for a decent amount of time. And invariably market factors such as economic announcements, interest rates, stock markets, etc. will impact the currencies in either of the nations.

You need to fully understand how the two economies operate and how these factors will impact your carry trading strategy. Whilst economic and political news releases may seem an exogenous factors to your trading plans, they may mean that you will have to close out prematurely an otherwise profitable carry trading strategy to avoid a loss.

3. Trade consistently. This is crucial in carry trading. This trading style involves holding long and short positions in a number of currencies. On most of them you will make a small amount of money every day (hopefully) and on some of them you will lose a small amount of money every day.

It's key that you are consistent and methodical by sticking to your plans day in and day out. If you decide to stop out of the strategy at a given point because you have accumulated losses, you may end up missing on a streak of profitable trades that would have brought you back into the black.

Carry trading is a special trading style compared to other strategies (forex robots, trend trading, scalping, etc.) and thus requires a slightly different approach mostly due to its longer trading horizon.

By implementing these 3 golden rules you will be a long way into the top 10% of the traders who profit trading forex, and you will be moving away from the 90% of traders who lose money.

Building a profitable forex trading strategy can be boiled down to two key factors - knowledge and testing. Visit TomorrowInTrading.com to benefit from expert reviews and gain advice on forex trading systems and forex signals.

Chapter 21

Turnaround Stock Strategy

In my earlier book "A Simple Guide To Investing in Turnaround Stocks", I referred to turnaround stocks as companies that are experiencing problems (hopefully short-term), and a lot of people are not willing to wait for those companies to recover.

Many people profess to be patient investors. In reality, not many can stand the heat of waiting their investments to turn around. You can identify such investors by asking them the reason why they invest on their stocks.

If they said that they invest because such and such has an exciting products in the pipeline, then they are most likely are not going to be patient with that investment.

If they admit that things look gloomy for their investment but, they believe that the company will turn that around with certain new executions, then they are patient investors. The truth is turnaround investors are patient investors.

They are willing to invest in a seemingly gloomy company with the expectation that things will change. No, it is not a stream of baseless hope. It is the patience to wait until the company can sort its mess out. That is hard to do, even for the most-seasoned turnaround investors.

The reason is simple. You invest in companies that people love to hate. You need to have strong conviction in order to stay on the course.

A lot of novice investors would buy some beaten down companies, only to sell it later due to emotional reasons. For instance, one folk might talked unfavorably about your company and you start to think that maybe he was right. After a while, another folk would talk some other terrifying things about your company and your mind started to tremble.

At that point, you could not wait to dump your investments in this stock and you were glad you sold the stock. That happens a lot and that is the reason why turnaround investors are rewarded so much.

Since not a lot of investors are willing to wait that long, the stock price can be bought at a much lower price than normal. This increases your potential return.

What are examples of turnaround investments? Hindsight is 20-20. But, let me give a few examples in the past. Altria Inc. was a good turnaround investment in the early 2000s. It was hit by lawsuits left and right and nobody is willing to buy a stock with 'tobacco' labelled in them.

Fast forward five years later, people still do not have a favorable view on tobacco but Altria stock price increase anyway. It is not a mere penny increase that we are talking about. Altria increases more than 200% since its low price in the year 2000. How about Seagate Technology in the middle of last year?

Analysts worry about the competition from flash disk which would cripple the hard-drive industry forever. The result? Seagate stock price rose almost 100% within one year. Not a bad return for investing in un-loved companies.

One final example would be the pharmaceutical companies. Concerns about their future pipeline depressed their stock price for much of 2005. In 2006, when it is clear that the pipeline is not all dry, stock price rose steadily to reflect that change.

You could have bought Merck shares in the $ 26 range last year and your investment would have gained 36% thus far. This is despite the uncertainty revolving around it. When the vioxx case is all settled, I think the stock price can rise approaching the previous announcement.

The key here though is to be knowledgeable about your companies and be patient. This way, you will have a strong conviction about your investment and you will not sell a potentially good investment portfolio.

That is not easy to do but you will get better at it with practice. For starter, our website features a regular commentary that gives you free investing idea about potential turnaround investment.

Wrap up

When you are considering investing your money on trading in the stock market, you may want to plan out your strategies and focus on practical forex training. Having a strategy in how to trade and deal within the stock market would require you to have the right information on what stock market trading entails.

That is why it is important to gather information that can allow you to understand how trading in the stock market is done and this goes the same for those that wish to learn forex trading.

The most important key to success in trading in the stock market is the right strategy, to have the right strategy you have to have the right knowledge of how stock market trading goes.

Having the right information and strategy, you will be able to use the stocks that you trade with as an instrument to acquire short term profits for yourself.

However, even if stock market trading is quite profitable, most beginners don't succeed well within the market because they lack the right strategy in order to avoid pitfalls that can lead you to spend all your investments and have nothing in return.

It is important that you establish a trading system that works for you when you start trading within the stock market. You should be comfortable on the level of the risks that you may be willing to take.

Most traders that have identified a set up where they are comfortable in executing find it easier to make a profit within the stock market. Keep in mind that even the best forex strategies will have a percentage of loss.

The trading system that you would wish to have and follow should be something that applies to your personality. Being comfortable with the way you trade can give you an added confidence in executing trades in the stock market.

When you are starting out, it is important that you immediately identify a trading system that would work well for you. It should be a trading system that can outweigh the losses that you may possibly make in your trading.

Knowledge is crucial in the stock market world and I would thus like to recommend the following books (that I co-authored) that will provide further insights into different investment strategies:

1. Winning with Growth Stock Funds
2. A Simple Guide to Investing in Turnaround Stocks
3. Options Trading Basics Explained
4. The Little Black Book of Out of the Box Investments

A last note from the author's desk: If this book has helped your understanding of wealth building through trading, would you consider rating it and reviewing it on amazon.com?